The
Woman on the
Bridge over the Chicago River

A BOOK OF POEMS BY ALLEN GROSSMAN

The
Woman on the
Bridge over the Chicago River

A BOOK OF POEMS BY ALLEN GROSSMAN

A NEW DIRECTIONS BOOK

Grateful acknowledgment is made to the editors and publishers of
various magazines and books in which some of the poems in this
volume originally appeared: *Boston University Journal, Canto, Georgia
Review, New Directions in Prose and Poetry 37, New Republic, Paris
Review, Partisan Review, Ploughshares, Poetry, Salmagundi.*

Manufactured in the United States of America
First published clothbound and as New Directions Paperbook 473
in 1979
Published simultaneously in Canada by George J. McLeod Ltd.,
Toronto

Library of Congress Cataloging in Publication Data
Grossman, Allen R   1932–
    The woman on the bridge over the Chicago River.
    (A New Directions Book)
    I. Title.
PS3557.R67W6 1979   811'.5'4   78–26802
ISBN 0–8112–0714–5
ISBN 0–8112–0715–3 pbk.

New Directions Books are published for James Laughlin
by New Directions Publishing Corporation,
80 Eighth Avenue, New York 10011

Contents

Foreword

The reader who takes up these poems will appreciate at once the altogether distinctive beauty of lines and phrases, often quite simple, elemental, and aphoristic lines and phrases, falling as unlaboredly on the page as light falls through a framing window on a wall. The prosodic or musical achievement is itself a rare one amid the poetries of the time, and no doubt like most fine art comes of long study and the intense exercise of choice. It can, of course, be distinguished only momentarily from poetic authority in general, which in this case is very firm.

The four other poetries to which allusion is made in this volume are those of Yeats, Crane, Stevens, and Plath. These are elevations named, I should think, by no particular design but representing a certain range, or kind. Of poetic life in this kind one feels this poet to be a participant and adept, with enough critical power to make the life of his own poems fully independent.

> Young life is breathed
> On the glass;
> The world that was not
> Comes to pass.

These lines, in an application that Joyce did not intend but wouldn't mind, seem to me merited by Grossman's pages.

The world in question is limited or defined by the writer's sense of what he can do authentically, and so should do, with his language. There are almost no mis-steps. The values are high. It is a world that for the most part exists outside and beyond, or before and after, the familiar modern diurnal one, and it shows that one, by implication, diminished upon a very large scale—a scale, however, given in terms of personal states of consciousness that correspond to scripture, nightmare, prophecy, and myth.

"What men seek for one another in literature," Grossman once said in an article, "is the safety which consists in telling a true story about the self, one which includes all the alliances of the self. And that must be a story which stretches from the origin of things to the end of things." This book is the partial telling of such a story, partial because limited or defined as I have remarked, and because the full story, to be continued, perhaps, would be all but illimitable. Some things here put me in mind of a phrase of late Stevens, "Profound poetry of the poor and of the dead." Here, among other things, is a poetry of the poor and of the dead, categories that are thoroughly understood to embrace both poet and reader.

At times they seem poems of great age, poems at the world's verge, at the verge of time. In their strange plenitudes and chasms they lament and suggest how what we know may be entirely too much for us. Now and again one feels the amazement of great vision—the amazement, and the pang and shudder. Then one comes upon poems that refuse the pride of the visionary, intimating a distinction, for example, between what is the case in one sense and what is the case only in the other sense of having been formed on the page by this intelligence at its somber pleasure. Or the poet offers speech in a differing voice as Allen Grossman, who teaches English at Brandeis, once had a nurse named Pat and later a colleague named Boime, a bad driver who got killed and who is rendered with sharp love and humor. Among the poet's tones, these are not the least beautiful.

ROBERT FITZGERALD

I

The Fame of Tears

THE WOMAN ON THE BRIDGE
OVER THE CHICAGO RIVER

Stars are tears falling with light inside.
In the moon, they say, is a sea of tears.
It is well known that the wind weeps.
The lapse of all streams is a form of weeping,
And the heaving swell of the sea.

                                      Cormorants
Weep from the cliffs;
The gnat weeps crossing the air of a room;
And a moth weeps in the eye of the lamp.
Each leaf is a soul in tears.

                         Roses weep
In the dawn light. Each tear of the rose
Is like a lens. Around the roses the garden
Weeps in a thousand particular voices.
Under earth the bones weep, and the old tears
And new mingle without difference.
A million years does not take off the freshness
Of the calling.

                  Eternity and Time
Grieve incessantly in one another's arms.
Being weeps, and Nothing weeps, in the same
Night-tent, averted,
Yet mingling sad breaths. And from all ideas
Hot tears irrepressible.

                    In a corner
Of the same tent a small boy in a coat
Sobs and sobs,

while under the Atlantic
Depth and Darkness grieve among the fountains,
And the fountains weep out the grieving sea.

O listen, the steam engines shunt and switch
Asleep in their grieving. A sad family
In the next house over shifts mournfully
About staining the dim blind. The boy looks up
As the grieving sound of his own begetting
Keeps on,
And his willow mother mars her mirror
Of the lake with tears.

                    It is cold and snowing
And the snow is falling into the river.
On the bridge, lit by the white shadow of
The Wrigley building
A small woman wrapped in an old blue coat
Staggers to the rail weeping.

                    As I remember,
The same boy passes, announcing the fame
Of tears, calling out the terms
In a clear way, translating to the long
Dim human avenue.

THE BOOK OF FATHER DUST

for Louis, my father

As God knows,

        the child sees,

                in middle age
The strewn windfall of the befallen.

             Today
I am reading the poems written when
I was a child (the cobalt tower text
Of Hart Crane; spinster Stevens' intricate
Book of needles; oracular Yeats,
Unkind). And I am writing a poem
(It *must* be this one) conceived when I
Was conceived—

       a war in the world wind.

.   .   .   .

I am from Louis, my father—the dust.

.   .   .   .

In middle age,

        the child sees,

             like an immortal,
His own begetting—the one shadow, and the faint

Sexual nuance of blown seed in the plumed
Shadow
Forty years ago—

                         this season, this hour,
This minute . . .

What was small is now large, what was young is
Now old, what was is now no thing.

            .   .   .   .

                                    —How did the
Dead soldiers, as they arose in the dark,
Put on their shoes? That is what they did, when
I was a child; they arose
And put on their shoes, somehow; and walked into
Their graves.

            But I came on as far as this
Bright morning, when all the gifts of the lineage
Were set down, as from
A spectral truck or vast galleon, warped
Silently in, out of the infinite, cricling, high
Oceanic roads—
Great boxes on the paving,

                         the cargo;

                                    scraped,
Burned, shattered, crazed, torn, shaken—dust.

            .   .   .   .

Amid the strewn befallen (this still
Morning of outcome)

              I marry Louis,
My author—the dust.
I take the dry yellow rubberband from
Around his wallet,

           and wind it on my
Book (in which
Will yet be bound by love in one volume
The scattered leaves of the whole world).

We are dust, Louis, and these are the lines,
God knows,

        which I must mend—
Conceived when I was conceived

               (bear with me)
At Xmas Lake,

     a war in the wind.

NOTRE DAME DE L'EFFROI

for Beatrice, my mother

On the way we pass The Convent of Mary's Fear. It is said that here
Mary stood, stricken with fear, when she saw her son led by the wrath-
ful inhabitants of Nazareth "unto the brow of the hill that they might
cast him down headlong." The nearby height is called the Precipice, or
the Leap of the Lord.—Vilnay

I have lost my little dear one,
Like a caterpillar under a milkweed leaf
In a field of milkweed.

                       First I fell asleep.
Then I went out into the field

                sleeping
And brushed the bees from under the fat leaves
Of the weed, bee after bee, until I saw him
With his black and orange mask, and false eyes.

I carried home the whole stalk of the bleeding
Tree to my city on the side of a hill—high,
Many chambered, with strange views

                      with steep streets.
There I kept him in the light.
And he wove a luminous green sack without a shuttle
And without a thread.
And without a hand he tied himself to the stalk
Of the milkweed.

I went away and labored in the room
With many doors. When I came home I could
Hardly look.
When I looked I could hardly see.

                              He was folded within
Like a written message. I was astonished.
It was the latter part of the summer.

Then he unstitched the sack
And staggered on six legs into the uncanny light
Dragging two dazzling flags packed crudely on his back,
Heavy with wet.

                    I held out my hand, and he
Mounted.
My tears coming, I said I did not know him.

He mounted down my arm to my wrist which I held
High above my head.

                              I have never felt so
Light——. Like a bird at the edge of a deep wood
I trembled on the steep sides of my town.
Where shall a woman turn

                              unless to the wild bees,
Unless to the ants, the worms?

And then he took flight, but did not disappear.
He rested on a twig for more than a minute,
Moving the creased flags on his shoulders
A little up and down.

                    And I saw that one was torn,
And drawn down, as by a wind—as by violence.

Where shall a woman turn unless outside
Where the graves are like fallen doors?

From high up thunder of a parade. *Hep*.
Hep.
And this spasm woke me. *Hep*. *Hep*. An armed

Chorus from bannered heaven was winding down
With light upon them, and empty eyes—
HIERUSALEM EST PERDITA.

                                          I have lost
My little dear one, like a caterpillar
Under a milkweed leaf in a field.

I have lost my child

BY THE POOL

Every dwelling is a desolate hill.
Every hill is a desolate dwelling.

The trees toss their branches in the dark air,
Each tree after its kind, and each kind after
Its own way. The wind tosses the branches
Of the trees in the dark air. The swimming
Pool is troubled by the wind, and the swimmers.

Even though this is not a tower, this is
Also a tower.

           Even though you are not
A watchman, you are also a watchman.

Even though the night has not yet come,
The night has come.

2

The Field

THE RUNNER

The man was thinking about his mother
And about the moon.

                It was a mild night.
He was running under the stars. The moon
Had not risen,

            but he did not doubt it would
Rise as he ran.

           Small things crossed the road
Or turned uneasily on it. His mother
Was far away, like a cloud on a mountain
With rainy breasts. The man was not a runner
But he ran with strength.

               After a while, the moon
Did rise among the undiminished stars,
And he read as he ran the stone night-scripture
Of the moon by its own light.

               Then his mother
Came and ran beside him, smelling of rain;
And they ran on all night, together,
Like a man and his shadow.

A PASTORAL

At that time the sheep called to him
From their wormy bellies, as they
Lay bloating in the field. He was
A pastoralist,
The schoolhouse hardly handsize
In a sky of flax.

He began
Then to keep the sayings of man
(The left hand writing; the right hand
Crossing out) farming the time by day
With a great rake
And in the evening hearing myths
Of the hurricane and the tornado
(Straws driven through glass),
And of the waking in the grave
(The sharp hands of brothers buried
Together).

In the deep night the rat-
Traps in the seed room broke the rat's
Back, and the rat called to him in
The next room over in a penetrating
Eloquent way.

In the parlor it was
Always deep night where the separated
Organs of the living slept in jars
(The lank goiter and the rotted
Appendix) awaiting the end-time
When the emasculated ram will rise
In the flax-blue sky
(Cold as the final bluing of a Sunday wash)

And all of us will know
The use in beauty of the whole body.

In the hay field was the beginning
Of knowledge:
Sour wine, the great rake hoisted
Toward the high sun-altar of the stack
And the hoist rope hauled out hard
(Like a greased whip of which the stories
Told were of the severing of limbs)
By two staggering teams—and the whole
Sun in its extreme tower of noon.

All he heard was violent and sad
But he kept on writing the sayings
Of man with his left hand, and sent
Them off in broken words, and waited
In the mortal field
Listening to the mice in the bottom
Of the stack.

        Now though the schoolhouse
Hangs like a stone over the field
Robed in its winding sheet as blue as air,
The shepherd hand of eloquence still keeps
And flashes
Out the sayings of the man—
And the other (the right hand of
Obliterating habit) sleeps.

THE FIELD, HER PLEASURE

Thunder over the field, voices
Of Memory, memory of the voices
And of thunder, thunder of memory
Over the field, slow after-speaking
To the lightning bolt, burdened
Interpreter of the quick, bright
Scratch.

And then the following
Spirit of the crepuscular
Small rain.

There is a man still
Sitting at the field's edge. The rain
Touches him here and there. And he
Sees her pleasure. It is rainy
Green. The lightning writes upon it,
And then the thunder in its time
Offers a meaning.

But the rain is
A kingdom with its own god
Over which the thunder batters
Like the "ach, ach" of strange dogs,
And birdsong rises from the grasses.

The man owes the field a name—
Perhaps, "Her Pleasure."
Behind him is the house where she
Is but the field is her pleasure.
In the field are the graves of strangers—
Who are the strangers buried in
The field of her pleasure?

                    In the dark
Field is a green stream,
A sort of track that with the fainter
Mazy tracks of other streams
Leads down to a standing pond
And the one willow.

                    Out of the fascination
Of her eye, he sees at last the green
Court of her whole love.

                    At the pond's
Edge she is there—
With a long pole, in the dawn light
Pulling the sunfish up.

A SNOWY WALK

I

The tongue grows looscr, the terms of praise
Slower, more inexact,

                   the day darker,
The rock cold—
And all the high terms of the wooing fallen
In a falling, a cadence.
I look backward
At you, my City of the Plain,
Iniquitous Sodom

               wife of some years,
As on a snowy path you walk toward the woods,
On the darker side

                where there is no sun,
And the snow breathes on your cheek,
The left,
Distance and intimacy growing together.

II

Seeing the beloved, first among fountains,
Then in the eelgrass

                  at the wide shore;
In childbed, also a wide shore;
On a snowy path—

Seeing what the light gives, and darkness takes away,
Salt seizes my eye.

III

I would be famous in your fields;
In your forests

        acknowledged
Huntsman;
In your deep lakes, rich gardens
Greeted by name;

        on your bright air
Unstream my banners—
Upon your snows, permitted pioneer.

FOR PLATH

I

My serious distress exhausts the mean device
By which I have survived you, and betrays
Your elegist born with you in a bad year;
But with his death still in his hand.

Going the obscure way by the light
Of a rich branch, under the Elm Tree
Fruitful of treasons, I draw my sword
Against the air. Easy the descent.

Great souls admire your careful wounds—
Clamorous, imperial, extinct in multitudes;
Before and after, up stream and down,
Tu Marcellus eris, numberless.

II

And see the gardens that they here devise
Who have no occupation now but love,
Gardens of great grieving, gardens of night,
The young forever moving their fair hands.

Hail! You who have picked the dexter way,
The Sacred Grove, inheritors of Persephone:
Jephthah's daughter, flowers in her hair,
Pallas, himself a flower, Galahad

And Isaac, gigantic questioners,
Greet now another by the right of wounds
Come down among you. Let this fame too
Be writ in the iron book and locked.

III

Madness is easy. But the reascent,
The closing of the wound, the wrestling match,
Heaven and Hell, honor and names, tears
And unoffending sleep, this is the labor

The matter of rising from this clear air
To that mysterious sun. The gates stand open.
Before me the White Elm and the Dread Fountain.
Who would drink? Who would revisit?

For what was given has been taken back
As in the aberration of starlight
And we hear it depart, like a wind rising,
Or a thunderous closing of doors.

IV

In this time of mighty funerals a vision:
Four children in four corners of the field,
Weeping white tears on the green grass
Without sorrow, and sleeping the starry night.

WINTER WHEAT

Going over the ground, walking as it were on water—
(This weather is tainted, and will not bear admiration)
The lost ones assert themselves in voices
Saying impossible things

Saying,
"The perfect lover holds himself from love,"
Calling to mind dead harvesters with freckled hands,
And the sun's ghost
Which is the sun remembered.

Under the withered gourd the shadow lingers.
Things forgotten but my own return
In voices:
"This is the marsh where the bloated lilly-root
Offends,"
"Let not my violence corrupt your love."

Here spin the mute fish singing,
"Nothing is obtained but of someone turned from us."

In Winter the sun's rays touched the ice,
And geese in flocks drifted toward the sun.
April found me going over the ground,
Seeking the grave of light
Sighing,
"Dead harvesters, dead harvesters"

Walking as it were on water.

PAT'S POEM

Semper dum vivam tui meminero—Erasmus, *De Copia Verborum*

This is a poem for my old nurse Pat—
Who had something wrong with her heart.

                        Pat had
An old mother with a tongue like a cow,
With whom I slept.
And she had a father, out of sight, named John
Who died slowly in a back bedroom
Like an abandoned wagon rotting in
A low wet pasture.

              Pat had a boyfriend
Whose best song was, "The Trail of the Lonesome Pine"
And a brother, Vince, who went to the war
Leaving a chained hound in the barn that howled
Four years straight night and day.

Most things Pat taught me were not true. What she
Did have a knack for,
Like skipping stones far out on the Lagoon,
I never could pick up. I don't know
What became of her . . .

                 Pat, failed nurse
With a too small heart, with all-consuming
Shadowy love I loved whatever
Behind that constant uniform of official
Imposture your freckled body was.

                  First teacher,
Out in Denver or wherever marriage
Or the grave has swarmed over your hiding,

I'll tell the world that I remember
Every nuance of your plain brown hair
In Summer light.

                              Because of you I cannot
Tie good knots.
Because of you, I weep at marching bands
Because of you, I cannot depart
From any shallow friend, tell truth, keep measure
Or make an end . . .

                              So I talk on to you—
And on and on—all through the sleepless
Afternoon, as a child might to a stain
Upon a shade.
When will you come to wake me, Pat. Oh, when?
The long room darkens, and your poem's made.

        .   .   .   .

Out of the disturbed house, always below,
Robed as in summer curtains, sheer and white—
The dog's howl stopped, the confounded knot tight—
Comes up the stair dark, silence, and the years.
Semper dum vivam tui meminero.
All my life long I will remember you.

TWO WATERS

I remember two waters. One leaf-brown
From the sink pump, soft, for washing not drink.
The other, clear, one pail a whole day's
Good light.

The brown water was rain, on dark days and
Windy nights of its own weight down fallen
On roof, or driven against wall,

                        sunk then
To cistern dark and darkened among leaves,
Heaved up by the hand pump to wash a man's
Dark hair—and thrown out like fluent grief
On the sheep-bitten funereal home field.

The other water they sent me out for,
Each staggering pailful like a great lens
Raised to a great light,

                    hard water, for drink.
No grief or ease in it, as I think now—
Unhindered brightness of the deep-stored snow.

ALCESTIS, OR AUTUMN: A HYMN

I

I have been throughout my life accompanied
By one who was a satyr to my stolid
Pain and strange virginity, and I
No longer know what reason brought him
To my side—although I know he now
Is gone; and I must either play his part
Or be diminished by the quantity of his
Peculiar savage being. After some years
A man becomes a mystery, and walks the bottom
Of the stream where no one meets, for all
Are one way flowing. After some time,
A man is claimed by time; and all his gods
Withdraw into the things from which they came—
Into wildflowers, and bright stones, and shells.

II

In mountain country they mark the graves with wood,
For they are weary of immortal mountains
And choose to lie beneath a different monument;
And in among tall grasses, and the fragile stems
Of birch most pale and aspen most afraid,
The wood nymphs come, and Venus of the dying world.
As this rain perishes upon the ground,
So I in you do pour my solitude,
Stern image of the world unviolated
Which to my sorrow I cannot forget.
Autumn is fiery—how glorious to die,
And glorious this rain which does not breed,
And glorious the sun which is so cold.
O Venus of the dying world—preside.

III

Simon Magus at last did marry Helen
Whom then the world did violate without
Respite, and in the lowest kind. And I
Who have looked upon her am not innocent.
Therefore, the leaves come down and lose themselves,
As lovers' words are lost, and disappear
No one knows where, though they were true.
What must be learned is how to love;
But where are the Schools, and Masters of the
Discipline? In this matter I have come
Too near to death. Think! No one
Is alive who knows, and we shall never
In our time grow nearer—
Though we marry, and our intimacy be profound.

IV

Of all the women whom I know it is
Alcestis I most passionately admire,
Who died for an unworthy man, being
Sure that love was death
And nothing more. Nothing is pure in
Nature. Not childhood, nor infancy
Nor the moment of begetting with its
Too many images. Uneasy in my
Labor, uneasy in my rest. In love
Distressed; and in my loneliness quite lost—
I walk out in this storm, as in a mind
Deranged but not unclean:
Alcestis is my dream, who died forever
And then rose—for three days mute and strange.

V

On Roman sarcophagi the satyrs are at ease,
Or slightly exercised in celebration
Of the marriage of Endymion and the moon—
So I would have it be when I lie down.
I will have had enough of immortality
When I die. There is eternity in love,
Eternity in sleep, eternity
In solitude. But death is free of life
Which has outlived reality. Thither
Let Alcestis come, when love is done
With her abused soul; and I shall worship
Her among the roots of trees, which are
The secret triumph of the long-lived oak—
That it from Hades thrusts up so high in air.

VI

There are in meditation certain meetings
Of more than one despair. O Venus, who presides
In Winter with more than common majesty,
And is the unreluctant paramour of war—
O Venus never kind, your gentlest touch
Is snow, and sweetest breath is snow-filled wind.
I live within a village of two streams;
Upon the one, the vessel of desire
Shrouded in bells and painted with an eye
Descends to where a confluent tide bears down
The vessel of the bride. The festival
Of meeting is a troubled water, and therein
The agony of kings is seen, and Troy—
Until the queen of love brings peace like ice.

VII

Beginning as astronomers, we are now
Declined to lovers,
Leaving the stars to find the eyes of animals
Wherein they burn with pure translunar fire.
Purest mother of perpetual mourning,
I am so wholly yours I am not mine.
The dead are restless; but the living feel
More pain—in their uneasy wandering.
There is no man betrayed except by you.
The heat of god delights you in the heavens,
While the unearthly fires of Winter
Devour here the firmament of the leaves.
Sweet lady, thy children are about to die,
And come to thee—the holocaust of history.

VIII

What can be thought more clearly than
This night is seen? I have prepared for
Winter a quiet room,
Where like the conscious wasp and autumn-
Driven fly, I shall inquire
What it means to die—until the Spring
Astounds me with its bells, or else the Winter
Deepens, and stars usurp the world.
I am given up to quiet, and the change of light.
Neither god nor goddess did create my solitude—
None can undo, therefore, that mighty work.
Deep within the wastes of mind by which I
Am possessed is insanity
Bestial, passionate, secular, and profound.

THE LOSS OF THE BELOVED COMPANION

Take away death, the last enemy—; and my own flesh shall be
my dear friend throughout eternity.—Augustine

Watching myself,

        naked,

              in the mirror—;
My penis thickens, erect. For what? It
Is the mind bleeding through the body
Into the light.

        The picture of my body
Raises my prick—
A stupid connoisseur—who thus salutes the
Image of his lack,

        reduced by half,

                trans-
Posed.

        Where will it end? They cannot meet.
Even as my helping hand arrives, it dies—

"Where are the objects of desire? The sheath,
The cradle, urn, and chalice of my sword,
My infancy, my ashes, and my wine?"

Thus, I stand (in a sense) quoting my own
Lines—; forging my signature to end the
Kindermord,

        weak flag of the seed's stream
Left in the void field,

                    the uncollected,
Early work of my right hand—

                              "This is not
Solitude peopled by phantoms,
Imagined things to which some good adheres;
But, rather, critical vacancy
In which desire wells, as from a sourceless fountain
And spills itself into a cloudy basin."

            .   .   .   .

Watching myself—,

                    impotent—,

                              in the void
Mirror of my early art, it comes to this—
Sex and the imagination are one.
Only the flesh (Hear me, now, father dust,
I have begun to speak),

                    only the flesh
Is painted with our likeness.

                         The gravity
Of the human image draws the heavy
Genital like an unseen earth—

                         (O that it
Could once *want* to disclose itself,
Touch itself, hold it-
Self open)

      —the mother-awesome, absence-
Narrow, passion-targeted, answering,
Empty X

"Living in my desire I feel the anxiety
Of endless fall. . . ."

     . . . .

Naked—;

      in the mirrors of these lines, my
Soul salutes
Our death, the hero flesh, dear, darker, dying
Elder friend,

     and blameless *hetairos*—,

        doomed
Charioteer who takes in hand the great
Engine of hope, and in my armor drives—
Cursing—under the
Mountainous, chill shadow of the citadel. . . .

What can a man say?

      rising now, alone, starting
The lineage of the left hand (I speak
To you in verse, so that when you hear me
You will *not* die),

     forging my own will
(It is enough) in the silver light—.
I shall say more.

REPETITIONS

I

Trying to remember a name,
acknowledging why I cannot find things,
thinking this has all happened before,

summoning the thought
that distance will make this moment

tolerable,
revising sentences
lying—

Katzenstein.

II

Crossing a field I saw, as it were, far off
a girl with body like a waterfall
and the face of a dog,

ferns with old leaves, and also
delicate new ones seen later—

fingers of two hands
laced

(The anniversary of a dream)

this way and that.

III

These signs on my return—
a tree branch falling in its time,
 lightning on the paving,

a bird nest
with many small birds on a low

hazel bough,
(On other planets, is the light so quick?)

a mirror-like

pool.

IV

All my life I repeat the same words
I got from a Maple tree one bright morning

spring 1942.
(There are very small moments in which the sun
rises and sets many times.)

They were like fruit or angels.

The tree had a fine shape, and has still.

People come from miles
around

to take pictures of it.

AFTER REPETITION

At once, illustrious Hektor took from his head the helmet,
and laid it all-shining on the ground.—*Iliad* VI

To place a poem among these poems
Without darkening the scene of
Placing the poem—

                  walking how lightly
To keep my foot from extinguishing the
Path, like a philosopher
Who makes his mind the only picture—
Not the mere poet broken in the
Saltmill of the manifest (the sea saying,
The shattering rock shore making it true)
But the mature
The self-determined maker

                  the *yogin*

                      whose walking

Lightly is a way—
Each good line a lineament—to make
More sure

        the slow overcoming of in-
Credulity

        the welcoming.

Leave mother and father to one another.
Leave off depicting. Avenge no one. Open

Your arms
            (when what I intended at first was

Only "The wind is in the house," and "The wind
Changes the place of light things")

       to his coming

                by the way opened
(The undarkened scene, the windless bridal
House serene)—undisguising

             setting down the
Battle mask
The plumed death's-head of nature on the ground.

(The image is death. Put off the image.)

The child shrieks

       as the gap displays

           his beauty.

THE ROOM

A man is sitting in a room made quiet by him.
Outside, the August wind is turning the leaves of its book.
The door is open, everything is disclosed, each leaf, all
    the voices.

The man is resting from the making of the quiet in which he sits.
The floor is swept, his books are laid aside open, his eyes
    are open.
All the leaves and voices are outside in the restless wind.

Soon he will rise, or take up a book, or someone will enter;
Or, perhaps, a leaf will come in across the threshold, or a voice
Will blunder through the room, blind and unanswerable on its
    way elsewhere.

But now the room is quiet as the man has made it.
Everything in its place is at rest inside the room.
And the man is at rest, seeing each leaf, and hearing all
    the voices.

3

Villa Malcontenta

THE CHILDREN'S HOUSES

Out behind the houses of the grownups
Are the houses of the children, and graves
Of small-boned animals, and churchly rocks
(Streamy, and Streaky, and the Jordan Marsh
Are rivers of the place); and mothers of real children,
Who are ghosts, and real mothers of ghost children
Finally fulfilling the great word "keeping."
No altars but rocks strewn here and there.
Nothing passes through fire, and fire passes through
All things, and the good-night bird goes "sip sip."

In the darkness the children are calling
To the mother in the nightdress who hears
The children calling, as she walks asleep
Calling to the children. "Save me," they cry.
"I am unarmed," she says. "I have no banner.
Truly! Darkness has no power at all."
But the children say their names, and the mother
Repeats them, "Smadar," and "Lena Luna,"
And "Alphonso," and "Jack." Listen! They are singing,
Even in this darkness, creational songs:

> *I have light at heart, young soldiers,*
> *I have heart-light; and my sisters,*
> *Our lionesses, have heart-light;*
> *And my brothers have heart-light,*
> *Our lions.*
> *Light's lions mount guard in light's house. . . .*

This is the vengeance of hindered creation:
Marriage of Behemoth, gigantic bride;
A deep nest for the dark wind; all things
Without anger; the sea in keeping, its

Soul raised up—a wave, an upland pasture,
A sweet face. As it was in the beginning
Before the hard rains came, and the face was
Worn and hollowed, and cruel absence made
The wave go down. As it was before rain ate
The face, and absence made the wave go down.

This is the vengeance of hindered creation:
Curing of the seed, and establishment
Of the landscape, and drawing down
Of the long dug of the rain—the revenge
Of ghost mothers of real children
And of the real mothers of ghost children
Finally keeping in their fragile lodges
The Sabbath of long kisses, and the great
Feast of heart-light, mothers and children
And no others, in the bannerless night.

> *Do you know I know you, young soldiers?*
> *Heart-light knows heart-light. And our brothers,*
> *The lions, know you;*
> *And our deep-throated sisters, the lionesses, who*
> *   know you*
> *Open their jaws.*
> *And the best song in the world will heal you—*
> *Heart-light.*

THE BALLAD OF THE BONE BOAT

I dreamed I sailed alone
In a long boat, a white bone;
Like a strong thought, or a right name
The sail had no seam.

The mast, and its shadow on the sea,
Fled like one high lonely tree
Bent with the weight of the wind-fruit sown
By the cold storm.

It was a dream of dignity
When I steered on that plated sea
With a seamless sail, and a boat like a bone,
In a fair time of the moon.

There was no rudder in the long bone boat,
The compass was a stone—
The air was empty of the deep sea gull,
And gone was the cry of the loon.

The sea and the sky were one dark thing,
The eye and the hand as cold.
Unbound was my hair, unbound was my dress;
Nothing beckoned or called

But the words of a song
That had death in its tune
And death in its changes and close—
A song which I sang in the eye of the moon,
And a secret name that I chose.

And this is the song: "Straight is the way
When the compass is a stone,
And the sail has no seam, and the boat is a bone,
And the mast is bent like a tree that bears
The wind-fruit of the moon."

And now I sing, O come with me,
And be at last alone;
For straight is the way in the dream of the boat
That is a long white bone.

THE COMET

The child and I waked in the dark.
Both cold
We walked the quarter mile to where the ridge
Gave us such sky
As was not hidden in the upper branches
Of the dying elms.

Winter had stopped both death and life in them.
I said,
"The sun will rise this morning South of East"—
Thinking,
This is no time for children. And yet it's not
The strangeness of the hour
But the promises it may not keep
That is the terror.
Thinking,
"We rise on stepping stones of our dead selves"—
Not rise, but grow
More haunted, being of our own too passionate
Last state the tomb or haunted house.

We came to see the comet—something
Promised.
The child in a long life might see it twice.
I stood
Proud pedagogue on a bitten hill, saying
"These are the stars,
And this gash—bleeding light—portendeth wars."

Thinking,
Wisdom is not seeing the meadow in one season
But in more than one season; not seeing
The world in one life, but in more than one life.
And then—
The dawn came on like the heating of iron.

THE HOLDOUT

If then the little girl whose ball it is
Were gay. But no, she is a sad, sad girl;
And will not play, but takes her ball, and goes.

How did this come about? Where is she gone?
Who gladly said, "O yes! You may say 'Yes'
To me," and threw the ball with a wild glance.

She has gone off where she will not be seen
To weep, because there are too many in
The game. What shall the man say? What shall he

Say, himself in tears, but "Play the game, sad
Little girl. We promise to play fair as
Fair, if you'll come back, and bring your ball?

Though it may seem to pass from hand to hand
And disappear, it will return to you
Like a wild look." "No, man in tears," she says

Out of the dark. "It's written in a book.
I won't come back—until the eagles shall
Forsake their hill and speech comes to the rook."

MY MARKMAN

I do not live by the sea but I have
   A friend who lives by the sea. On him
      The wind sheds images of the far shore

When he walks in the wind. On me the wind
   Does not shed images, but I know of
      The far shore because he tells me of it.

Where he walks the Monarchs in their season
   Come across tacking and swooping over
      The wave crests from the far shore, and then over

The salt marsh and the sea grass, one by one
   Battering toward sleep in the Sierra Madre.
      Also whole days come to him on the wind

To which he gives a name, such as Storm Day
   Or Wash Day or Death Day. He marks each one
      With a clear mark, a term. In Winter he

Takes account of the six wings of the snow.
   On the far shore where gulls nest in the clearness
      Of his thinking are treasuries of snow

And the wild horns from which spill butterflies.
   I love my markman who lives by the sea
      On whom the winds shed images he knows

I love him for the waking and for the time,
   The whole days, and for the Monarch on the
      Wind road to the mother mountain of sleep.

O GREAT O NORTH CLOUD

Friend of long standing, the wind-shaken rose,
   The shingle raised up and writhen like a back-
      Blown wing, our whole house of friendship
         A vessel twenty years at sea, the sea

Itself, graces and torn powers, and beasts under it,
   Far shores and delicate grasses great and small
      Risen as if summoned by a unique spasm of the moon . . .

It is mid-afternoon of the last Summer month
   And the children are calling to others a long way off.
      The seed has taken hold, and the seedsman has returned
         With his long knife, his team, and his great wain.

The sullen wasp is winding up his hive.
   All but the latest flowers are in bloom.
      Friend of long standing, the wind-shaken rose
         Knocks and will not be tied,

And a great cloud rises, northward of many lights,
   Like a dark stone upheld. O great, O north cloud, speak!
      "Winter," it says. "Winter, winter, winter."

THE SALT TRADE

The salt merchants beat drums to signal their arrival. They arranged their salt in piles and went back out of sight. The gold traders then came out of their mines and caves with their gold and put the amount they were willing to offer beside each pile of salt. Then they went out of sight. The salt merchants returned and considered the offers. The process of bargaining continued until the salt and gold traders were both satisfied.

Sometimes the gold traders were in such need of salt that they were willing to pay as much as two weights of gold for each weight of salt. At times, when they could not get any pure salt they existed by using the ashes of plants, and by eating the meat and drinking the blood of such animals (and humans) as they could capture.

They knew from personal experience that they could live without gold but not without salt.—William W. Boddie, *The Silent Trade of Timbuktoo*

I

Blue fallen Jacaranda, the night rains, sleep
Almost to extinction—
And then desire (the mourning dove, infants
Suspiring in flutes) and tall sheep with brilliant
Garbage tied in their long hair the shepherds
Summon with a curse. The pounding mattock
Of the sullen gardener begins to wake you,
Under your afghan, your hound still folded
At your feet like sleep. The salt light enters
My eye and lodges—one grain at a time.

II

All day, and much of the night, my thoughts come in,
Burdened, silent, cruel—salt laden
Camels to Timbuktoo. Foul, relentless
Caravans from the North,
Resting infrequently, and without plan,
At unknown stations, transgressing untaxed
The boundaries of the great kings of the way
Bring in the salt.
The wind blows but the salt camels come in,
Thousands upon thousands till death end the need.

III

There are great thinkers, as there are bright stars.
They are not more to me than rain blurring
The window, and less, by dim magnitudes,
Than your averted eyes.
But the camels and the camel men bring salt,
Killing sleep with the harsh manners of the North
And the vile songs of Tripoli.
Salt is like thinking—strong savor of rock—
That cannot be put off,
When the rain stops, and the great stars blaze down.

IV

Eye blinded by seeing, market of tears,
To Timbuktoo comes down what is, that pit,
That hollow, where all things come down, and stunned
In rapture turn to salt. Cowries and gold
We give, embroidery of all flowers,
A sad nation of traders
Feeding its sad salt hunger with the tales
Of the camel men. They sing what they know,
Leaving me
Poorer, and in a world less reconciled.

V

The winds blow. Rains shift to the South—
And not return.
A sort of patience, and a sort of light;
Half light, and wrathful patience without peace.
The lions in their dream come down to salt
From the high Mountains of Air. Where are you?
How could I lose you in so small a house?
Either you are in the kitchen,
Or in the garden, or lying down under
Your afghan, or gone away with your hound.

VI

They go, deadly visions, the salt trade done,
Up the wind's black track, leaving the salt light.
In the seared eye of Timbuktoo, wind's weir,
I stir and startle at thought's ebb and cease:
To identify the objects in the landscape,
That gives pleasure—
The manifest, and the unmanifest, tree;
The dim salt cliff, so womanlike; the barren
Hill and shade;
The caves of absence by the estranging tide.

VII

Hysteria at the crossroads. Real tears.
The end of no thought, but thought's end—last salt.
Where are you? Gone with the rain's romantic
Hue and cry. At the moment of tears, found gone.
Hysteria at the crossing
Where two ways thunder in contestation.
Shall I leave the city Timbuktoo, where
Lions roam the lion city? Sister,
Return
And let me see you, as the light declines.

NIGHTMARE

In the dark bottom of his head there lay
A severed head.

                 He saw it when he closed
His eyes to sleep. And when he opened them
It lingered on things like a stain.

                      He paused
To find a moderate term for what he saw—
Things among themselves at first seemed
Quietly known to one another, and then
For no reason he could understand, flung
Themselves across the singular abyss
In shreds—burned and died to be perceived by him,
Standing a moment on the balcony.

In short, he saw that everything he saw
Was broken.

              And then the night formed whole
With all its stars about the man discovering
The brokenness of things.

                 After a while
He went down to the street, and walked along
An embowered path.

                 Someone who had been sitting
On a bench since sunset stirred impatiently
As if to rise as he approached him
In the early morning light. But the two
Men turned away from one another. They were
Like swans which avoid touching
Like the species of swans which does not touch.

THE FOVEA

The fovea (that little pit) a grave . . .

It was not death, the thundering in
the weir
but the untidyness of the cemetery
"its not being kept up"

she feared

lying down under pages foxed and torn

TERRA   terrible
no longer the theme of tears but tears

An island inundated twice a day
a city twice a year rising from the sea with weed
wrapped about the housetops

The great owl hawked at his tears like mice

ADAM'S TEARS
and first light enters picking its way
over corpses, mostly children

and some bodiless cries and some bodies without
mouths that never cried or spoke
and some babbling at ear or anus

WHAT MUST BE IS

The physician with poisoned hands attends

A day's messages

THE LADY OF VILLA MALCONTENTA
DEPARTS WITH THE DAWN LIGHT

Tell the king, the fair wrought hall has fallen to the ground. No longer
has Phoebus a house, nor a prophetic laurel, nor a spring that speaks.
The water of speech is quenched.—The last utterance of the Delphic
oracle in reply to a question of Julian the Apostate

In the debates of the child who failed to thrive
With the boy struck by lightning,
Over which the bandaged man ("necrosis of the face")
Presides, does poetry enter in?

                 O, no.
The doctor at night, not hearing the first birds,
The gray faced mother-doctor
In the silence of not hearing the pain-song
Plucks a hair from the child's lip.

                 In the corner
By the mirror, the grieving mother-doctor,
Audience of all song,
Caresses her breasts and says, "Nothing is enough."

The lost face of the man without a face appears
And disappears in the corners of the mirror.
The mother-doctor caresses her breasts, and then
Wearily opens and closes her blond braid,
Averted from the flickering revenant.

"Agnes," says the struck boy, "from being
Much too much drawn up my penis aches.
Agnes, my heart stopped, out of your keeping."
Thus, on the limb of darkness, at the edge
Of the great space of the room, the struck boy
Empties his left hand of the argument,

And his right hand remembers its lost uses—
How taken up, how moved.

                              Where is the voice
The mother-doctor loves? The voice of
The master of the voices,
Toward which she would look round, did look, uncovering
The mirrors, stood up laughing, laughed, taking
Her hair down, shaking out the pins. It would
Say, "Beatrice," if her name was Beatrice,
"Apollo's house is fallen."

The bandaged man whose face was taken away
Concludes the sessions, "Pain does not heap up
Even where it most abounds."

                              A wind shakes him
And Dawn falls into the great hall. "Master,"
He says, "It is so long, and long. . . ."
The damaged ones murmur along the limb of
Darkness, like stormed fruit.

For a moment, at first light, nobody wants
The grieving mother-doctor. There is no one
Alive, or dead, or being born in the
Great dream house. For a moment, she has vanished
On the blond arm of the stranger, leaving
A slight discoloration in the rainy light—
"Perpetua,   . . . petua, . . . tua, . . . tua,
. . . tua"—and cruel unwriting in the air.

ABISHAG THE IMPENITENT

Of the captivity of the beautiful creature,
The golden chains sing: "O, Garlanded."

First, the chickadee, early on, sucking and blowing;
Then, the other birds, dividing the waters from the waters;

Then the dawn, a barred and stippled animal;
And the hunter with his hounds which haunt

The wild ways of the sun's bound like bells—
And the dew goes up like long horns.

Cold in every part, and unaroused by what I am—
In a fit of my abstraction, the night ends.

4

Victory

THE THRUSH RELINQUISHED

One night there was no moon, and never had been.
In the space where the moon was

                              the weather
Stopped, everything happened for
The first time.

                  I cannot imagine space
As it then was, the cradle unrocking
In the tideless air.
The man stopped, the shadow vanished,
There was nothing to read.

In their yellow groves the midnight villas
Went dark, as if the timid sleepers put
Out the fear lights, the dark being no more
"The dark." Patience in me ceased to betray
Itself by tears.

The poet is dead, and from his stare released
The stars weary of dance divest themselves
Of countenance.

                  No poetry tonight. Death tonight.
The thrush relinquished, my hand is in the open.
I can see every way.

VICTORY

There is a radiance about the bed,
From which I turn to take account of the
Radiance, the still space of the bed.

The household is filled with unborn children
(Some will be born. Some will not be born.)
Chattering on the stairs in the two languages
Of the born and the unborn. I sleep reading
The bright day backward like a Hebrew book.

Today, I saw the whole body of ocean
From a hill. First I looked away. Then I
Looked, and there it was.

                    The children were playing
On the rocks. There was a woman I knew
Down there. Then I saw the whole ocean,
And we were no more scattered
Like swallows, or flowing from the broken
Hill like shards, but the swallows as they were
Before the scattering.

              I love you more.

The bed is a mountain, and the light is
The magnanimity of the mountain,
In the still space of the room where I sleep.
On the mountain we met a young hunter
Who asked the way of us, and did not wait
But strode off without the answer in another

Direction.
                    We climbed the iced flume
Carrying the answer to the grim rage
Of the top, where the whole earth stands, in the
Peril of high seeing—bed and abyss:

Birth bed, and sex bed, night storm bed of the
River dream, death bed of the born (despair
Of the unborn). I have come up now
Into the cloudy stone, and I have seen the earth;
And I have seen the sea, in the magnanimity
Of mountain light.

                    From the summit voices
Seemed to come. But when we climbed up there,
Our beards frozen, eyes turned from the wind, we
Found no one, and I had this thought, "She will
Never come. Not to him, not to me—alone of men."

And so if I bind on Apollo's phylacteries
I do it now to tell the plain truth.
Come, I will stop this talking. That is what
This voice inside you I am saying means.
Let us draw the black ship down to the divine sea—
Set the purple sail to the great death winds
Of the South, and empty
Out of the burden of our singing, you and I.
This is the whole ocean. Also the end.
After the wind stops,

                    the sound of the wind.

In the still space of the bed, I dream
The poet died. He had great difficulty
Dying.
He was reading a book about dying.
And then he died.

                  And the woman Victory
Unbound the strap from his forehead
And the other strap from his arm, and laid
Them by.

And then she rested from her triumphing.
She unbound her breasts, and she rested.

A SALUTE TO THE HERO PAIN

Consummatum est

The woods are falling.
The flowering hedges drain toward the vanishing point.
Crying out in a loud voice, the lichen
Blazes

      and towers.
You,
The unborn, still triumphing
Turn.

Who walked this way, his face unlovely, the whole
Man an offense to the eye?

                        The garden filled
With snow, empire
Withered.

        Death changed his
Note.

PAIN—
(These waters I sail were never sailed before)
There is nothing like it.

             O, not pearls!
Spoor not eagles nor mole can follow,
Path pathless, even to thousands: the soul's
Soul from the scabbard limbs
Drawn forth.

Out of the vanishing point—
Formless, in pain—

                          comes the hero.
The birches hurl down their boughs.
The horn of the lichen blazes

And towers.

BY THE SEA

Out of its pit the sea labors to move.
It cannot for the storm's torment rise
Or shake the tempest from its mouth and eyes—
Held down by something like a weighted net.

But far upon it, intricate and moved,
A great wave—nebular, bannered green and blue,
Raised up, scribbled with histories—burns through
Its destiny, fulfills a perfect year.

Thus, the escaped hues of earth and heaven
Over the shoulders of this slave,
Return—as if by chance—the dark world's look
From the high, morning windows of a wave

To fishermen bound to the bitter mill,
Salt-blind, fighters with nets, subdued to kill.

THE DEPARTMENT

Siste, viator

Bereaved of mind by a weird truck,
Our fraternal philosopher
To whom a Spring snow was mortal
Winter—a wild driver in the best
Of cases, on the margins of
Communicability—exchanged a bad
Appointment in New Hampshire
For a grave in the Jewish Cemetery
In Waltham, Massachusetts. Across
The street from the University
And nine feet from Philip Rahv
He keeps his hours, perished
With little fame.

His name was Boime.

"A very heavy business, Grossman"
He would have said,
If he had heard his own death going
The way it did.

Immortality
Was our Summer debate. But in the snow's
Confusion blurring definitions
Darkened into mortal blows. Consider
The wit
Of circumstance which made that mind—alive
Unwriting, and naive—
Record its own demise on paper
As a flat brain wave.

Who speaks for
Boime for whom
The University found just this much
Room?

His subject was the violence
Of mind, and the duplicity of his kind.
There was a wound, he thought, deeper
Than doubt where love

could enter, or
Look out—
Weary of the faithless civil compromise.
But that was not the wound of which he died.
He was a lousy driver who got caught.

An idle woman looked out on his burial
From her window
In the salmon colored house,—

a disharmonious fact
Between the cemetery and South Street—
Sitting on a bed.
Nothing can be said, except

the passionate
Theorist is dead. In death he was
Unclear—

His aged father, like a gouged up root;
The bitter wife; the child of five
Who wondered how his dad would ever
Get out of that box alive;
The bearded bandits who cranked him down
Know as much as I do,

or anyone.

He left his work unfinished. Whether
It was good or bad nobody knows—
It was not done.

           Somebody is digging
On your grave, dear Boime,
Who in that snowfall, when you died,
Was farther South than you,
Better employed.

           Your name is
Penciled in now on a tinny bracket
By a casual hand. A baby
Has been buried at your side.

           Since you
Died
It is the second Spring,
And nobody has set up your stone.

           God
God what a big
Thought, Boime, you carried into middle age—
Fat gladiator, treacherously caught
By a suffocating thin snow, chained
To a careening metal cage.

I am digging on your grave, like a starved
Dog burying a fact—

           If I say, "Boime, you
Were abstract,"

           then with a great sweet
Smile, even from among the dead,
Who don't know anything, he will reply,

Leaning a little toward the Summer

                                  under
His unbalanced cloudy load,
And with his lovely gesture of the hand,
"Grossman, you do not understand
The place of theory.

                Get off the road."

A CLOUDY NIGHT

He resolved to say nothing he did not know.
It was a cloudy night.

                  A half-formed moon
Inside its dirty atmospheric sack

Uttered no intelligible sound. The oak leaves
Just rearranged themselves, like a lineage
Preparing to receive a new soul.

                      That night
He saw that the moon was his near neighbor—
A human moon.

                So many things entered in
The following a simple track under
A human moon—the cold, the dark, the wet

Air—that at first he could say nothing. Then
The words that came were more a history
Than a song. . . . At last, the moon was shaken
Out of its sack.

                He sat down by gleaming
Moonlight in the odd angle at which he
Found himself, and thought.

                  A singular thing
Came to mind—a perfect countenance with a moon-
Like mark on its brow.

When he said to the moon,
"I want to take whatever you are to me
Inside me," his mouth fell silent

Like an unbandaged wound found healed.

VILLANELLE OF KEEPING

"I have become Death, shatterer of worlds."
(You do not read, I do not write this verse.)
Battered by absence the tablet earth endures.

Everything will perish, everything that lures—
Lo! The cold black cloud, the phallic whip, the curse:
"I have become Death, shatterer of worlds."

The stallion Void dismounts. The seed is hurled.
("There is nothing like me in the universe.")
Battered by absence the tablet earth endures.

Out of the maelstrom a howling infant crawls,
Hunting the blind breast of its idiot nurse.
"I have become Death, shatterer of worlds—

I change all things." The earth remains, and cures.
(Everything will perish, except this face.)
Battered by absence the tablet earth endures

Storms of unwriting; and the lines still bless
The narrow light, the morning star in tears.
"I have become Death, shatterer of worlds."
Battered by absence the tablet earth endures.

LAMENT FRAGMENT

Go down

(Forsaking the lagoons of bridged Atlantis)

To the mid-Atlantic ridge

                        where are the crazed
Magnetic fields and roped sheets, and stains
(The disordered fabric of the volcanic
Bed chamber) and the gigantic vermicular
Testimonies

            and stare upon the great
Principle of the solid world—the original
Torment trace.

                Go down, for down is the way.
And grapple one stone syllable
Of all that frozen love's discourse
Onto an iron dredge

             and on it rise
(Borne on the enormous weight of its desire
For light and the air)

              until it explodes
Upon the deck amid the astonished crew.

Then empty out the nets disposed about
Your person, and fill them with the pieces
Of that one vast syllable

                              and carry them
To Cahokia in East Saint Louis, where
My father was born who is dying now

(He was an honest man—mute as stone)

Place them on the top of Monk's Mound

(Go you. I am his son. I have no words.)

                                        and let

Them off like a siren.

THE LECTURE

Place a man in the center, and he becomes
The man who has prepared for a lifetime
To answer, and now is ready.

                              Sometimes,
There are trees at the edge of the clearing,
More often a sea. He talks on and on.
And his voice is carried up by the thermals
At the sea's edge, or down among the dark
Anfractuous trees, and the textile moss.
The lesson is staggering, and the examples
Come to hand like sheaves in a great harvest.

But, in fact, there are no trees, there is no sea,
And the center is some eccentric region
Of a bed or a room, and the question
Is the half-demented glance of a child,
Or a blurred silence on the telephone,
For which the man who has prepared a lifetime
Is ready.

       But the harvest is a great harvest.

After a long time, the voice of the man
Stops. It was good to talk on and on.
He rises. And the sea or forest becomes
A level way reaching to night and the thunder.

But, in fact, there is no night. There is
No thunder

Index of Titles and First Lines

Some New Directions Paperbooks

Complete descriptive catalog available free on request from
New Directions, 80 Eighth Avenue, New York 10011   † Bilingual